FUN SONGS
for the early years

Animal songs

Linda Mort

Credits

Author
Linda Mort

Editor
Jane Bishop

Assistant Editor
Kate Element

Series Designer
Anna Oliwa

Designer
Geraldine Reidy

Cover Illustration
Chris Simpson

Illustrations
Louise Gardner

Music setting
Sally Scott

All songs supplied by CYP.

Text © Linda Mort 2005
© 2005 Scholastic Ltd

Designed using Adobe InDesign

Published by Scholastic Ltd
Villiers House
Clarendon Avenue
Leamington Spa
Warwickshire
CV32 5PR

www.scholastic.co.uk

Printed by Bell & Bain

1 2 3 4 5 6 7 8 9   5 6 7 8 9 0 1 2 3 4

British Library Cataloguing-in-Publication Data
A catalogue record for this book is available from the British Library.

ISBN 0 439 96494 6
ISBN 9 780 439 96494 4

The right of Linda Mort to be identified as the author of this work has been asserted by her in accordance with the Copyright, Designs and Patents Act 1988.

All rights reserved. This book is sold subject to the condition that it shall not, by way of trade or otherwise, be lent, hired out or otherwise circulated without the publisher's prior consent in any form of binding or cover other than that in which it is published and without a similar condition, including this condition, being imposed upon the subsequent purchaser.

No part of this publication or CD may be reproduced, stored in a retrieval system, or transmitted, in any form or by any means, electronic, mechanical, photocopying, recording or otherwise, without the prior permission of the publisher. This book remains copyright, although permission is granted to copy pages where indicated for classroom distribution and use only in the school which has purchased the book, or by the teacher who has purchased the book, and in accordance with the CLA licensing agreement. Photocopying permission is given only for purchasers and not for borrowers of books from any lending service.

Acknowledgement

Qualifications and Curriculum Authority for the uses of extracts from the QCA/DfEE document Curriculum Guidance for the Foundation Stage © 2000 Qualifications and Curriculum Authority.

Every effort has been made to trace copyright holders for the works reproduced in this book, and the publishers apologise for any inadvertent omissions.

Contents

Introduction 5

Pets

Little Mousy Brown 6
Music 6
Lyrics 7
Activities 8
Photocopiable 9

Little Topsy Rabbit 10
Music 10
Lyrics 11
Activities 12
Photocopiable 13

Little Miss Muffet 14
Music 14
Lyrics 15
Activities 16
Photocopiable 17

Farm animals

I Went to Visit a Farm One Day 18
Music 18
Lyrics 19
Activities 20
Photocopiable 21

Horsey, Horsey 22
Music 22
Lyrics 23
Activities 24
Photocopiable 25

I'm a Duck 26
Music 26
Lyrics 27
Activities 28
Photocopiable 29

Hey, Diddle Diddle 30
Music 30
Lyrics 31
Activities 32
Photocopiable 33

Two Little Chickens 34
Music 34
Lyrics 35
Activities 36
Photocopiable 37

Animal songs

Contents

Chook, Chook 38
- Music 38
- Lyrics 39
- Activities 40
- Photocopiable 41

Fieldmice 42
- Music 42
- Lyrics 43
- Activities 44
- Photocopiable 45

Two Little Dicky Birds 46
- Music 46
- Lyrics 47
- Activities 48
- Photocopiable 49

Wild animals

Down in the Jungle 50
- Music 50
- Lyrics 51
- Activities 52
- Photocopiable 53

Nellie the Elephant 54
- Music 54
- Lyrics 55
- Activities 56
- Photocopiable 57

When Goldilocks Went to the House of the Bears 58
- Music 58
- Lyrics 59
- Activities 60
- Photocopiable 61

The Bear Went over the Mountain 62
- Music 62
- Lyrics 63
- Activities 64

Introduction

Using animal songs

From the first moment when a young baby touches a soft toy animal, most children are fascinated by all kinds of animals. This is reflected by the enormous popularity of children's animal songs, from gentle lullabies about pussycats, and reassuringly familiar songs about the universally beloved teddy bear, to lively action songs about pets, farm animals and wild animals. Songs about pets help children develop positive feelings about looking after animals, while songs about farm animals teach an understanding of the relationship between human beings and animals, as well as knowledge about a rural way of life, both now and in the past. Songs about wild animals help children learn about animal behaviour, and also to come to terms with worries and fears. From the simplest songs based on animal noises, all animal songs foster the development of role-play, pretend and fantasy play, as children love to move like, and pretend to be, animals. Many animal songs can also be used to teach counting and sorting skills, especially when reinforced with related play using model animals.

How to use this book

This book contains ideas for reinforcing, developing and extending the 15 engaging animal songs on the accompanying CD. There are two double-page spreads for each song: the musical score for each song is printed on the first double-page spread, together with simple instructions for suggested actions. The second double-page spread for each song contains two sections, 'Sharing the song' and 'Activity ideas', plus a photocopiable activity for 14 of the songs. 'Sharing the song' suggests the learning concepts that can be developed through the song, together with appropriate themes. Ideas for introducing each song are given, as well as suggestions for appropriate times during the day for playing the song. Suggestions for optimum group sizes and ideas for props are also given. The 'Activity ideas' section consists of activities to develop the songs' concepts and themes. The range of songs covers all six Areas of Learning of the Foundation Stage. Every song is linked to a Stepping Stone and an Early Learning Goal.

How to make the most of the songs

Introduce each song by playing the CD, more than once if possible. Invite everyone to sing along to the words and to join in with the actions. Whenever possible, use soft toy animals or glove puppets to 'lead' the singing. It is a good idea to play the songs outside, using a CD player in battery mode. Encourage the children to learn how to operate the CD player independently to enable them to enjoy the songs as they play. Occasionally, play a song quietly in the background as children become engrossed in an activity related to the song.

Provide a range of percussion instruments so that the children can play along to the songs and create prop boxes to accompany the rhymes, containing dressing-up items and other props that can enhance the children's enjoyment of the songs.

Areas of Learning

PSED Personal, social and emotional education
CLL Communication, language and literacy
MD Mathematical development
KUW Knowledge and understanding of the world
PD Physical development
CD Creative development

Pets

Little Mousey Brown

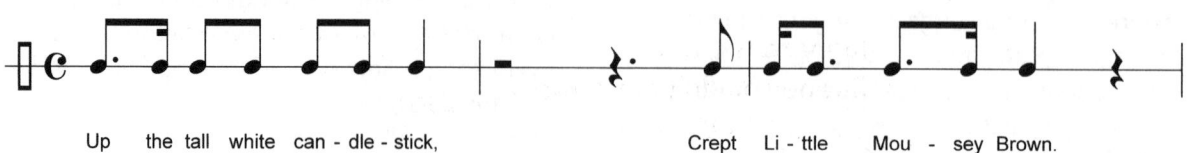

Up the tall white can-dle-stick, Crept Li-ttle Mou-sey Brown.

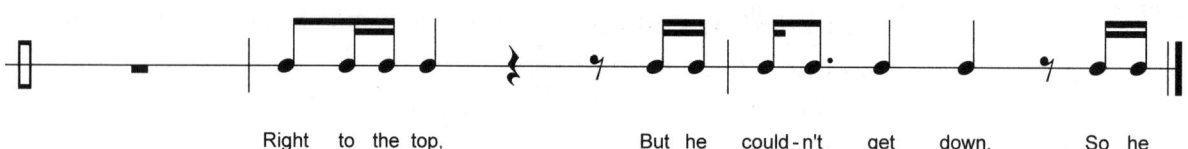

Right to the top, But he could-n't get down. So he

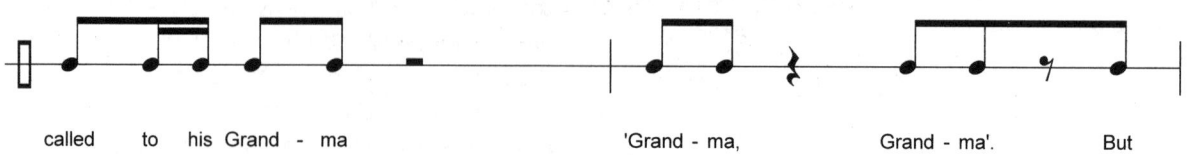

called to his Grand-ma 'Grand-ma, Grand-ma'. But

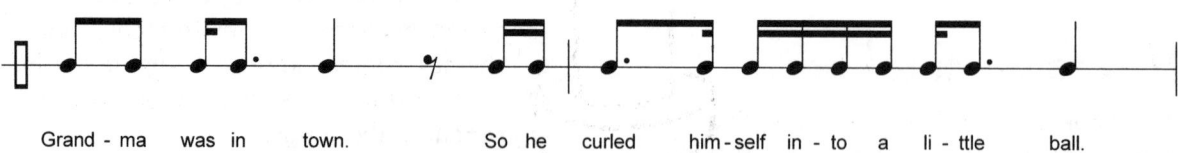

Grand-ma was in town. So he curled him-self in-to a li-ttle ball.

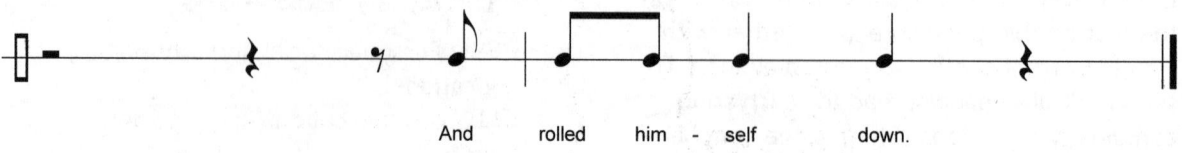

And rolled him-self down.

Little Mousey Brown

Up the tall white candlestick
Crept little Mousey Brown.
Children make creeping finger movements upwards, with one hand.

Right to the top,
But he couldn't get down.
Children look downwards, in mock alarm, with eyes wide open.

So he called to his Grandma,
'Grandma, Grandma',
But Grandma was in town.
Children open both arms and hands wide in 'problematic' gesture.

So he curled himself into a little ball
And rolled himself down.
Children make 'rolling' movement with both hands rotating over and under each other.

Pets

Little Mousey Brown
How to use this song

Learning objectives

Stepping Stone
Explore malleable materials by patting, stroking, squeezing, pinching and twisting them.

Early Learning Goals
Handle tools, objects, construction and malleable materials safely and with increasing control. **(PD)**

Group size
Four children.

Props
A candlestick.
Mice made from brown malleable material.

Sharing the song

Use this song to develop concepts of rolling movements, feeling nervous, grandparents and past times. Appropriate themes can be 'Ball games', 'Feelings', 'Families' and 'How we used to live'. Children will enjoy reciting this rhyme as they explore malleable materials such as play dough.

Introduce the rhyme by holding up a small 'mousey brown' you have made from any brown, malleable material, and a candlestick. Play the CD and ask everyone to join in, making the appropriate actions.

Next let the children each make their own 'mousey brown' using any available brown, malleable material.

Give everyone a copy of the photocopiable sheet and ask the children to point to the mouse hole in the skirting board.

Ask everyone to sing the song again, as they make their 'mouse' 'creep' up the candlestick in the picture, curl up at the top and then roll down.

Activity ideas

● Ask if anyone has ever felt nervous (a little bit frightened) about something, perhaps when they have climbed to the top of a climbing frame. Ask the children to say what it felt like inside, and what they would say to someone also feeling nervous to help them. Talk about how hedgehogs curl up when they are nervous or frightened. **(PSED)**

● Talk about grandparents together and make a list of the different names the children have for them. Talk about what the children enjoy doing with their grandparents and make a large book about it. (Remain sensitive to individual childrens' family circumstances.) **(CLL)**

● Find pictures of other traditional rhymes involving candlesticks or mice, such as 'Wee Willie Winky', 'Jack be Nimble' and 'Hickory Dickory Dock'. After reciting each one together, ask everyone to experiment by adapting the words to include the name 'Mousey Brown', for example, 'Wee Willy Winkie runs through the town, upstairs and downstairs, like little Mousey Brown!'. **(CLL)**

● Explain that the farmhouse kitchen on the photocopiable sheet shows a kitchen from a long time ago. Say that there were no electric lights then, and that people had to use candles to light their rooms. Make a display of candlesticks, preferably old ones if possible. Point out and talk about all the other old-fashioned features in the picture such as the range and ask the children to think about what is different in their own kitchens at home. **(KUW)**

● Let everyone make small balls from silver foil and devise simple tracks on a table or floor, with bricks. Let the children push or flick the balls with their forefinger. **(PD)**

Little Mousey Brown

Pets

Little Topsy Rabbit

Children put both hands upright on top of head, like rabbit ears.

Little Topsy Rabbit had a fly upon her nose.
Children point to their nose.

Little Topsy Rabbit had a fly upon her nose.
Little Topsy Rabbit had a fly upon her nose.
She flipped it and flopped it and it flew away.
Children gently flip an imaginary fly away from their nose, then stretch out their hand to indicate the fly flying away.

Shiny nose and curly whiskers.
Point to nose and rotate fingers to make curly whiskers
Shiny nose and curly whiskers.
Shiny nose and curly whiskers.
She flipped it and flopped it and it flew away.

Pets

Little Topsy Rabbit
How to use this song

Learning objectives

Stepping stone
Show care and concern for others, for living things and the environment.

Early Learning Goal
Consider the consequences of their words and actions, for themselves and others. **(PSED)**

Group size
Five children.

Props
Soft toy rabbits.
Paper 'flies' on string.

Sharing the song

Use this song as an opportunity to develop the concepts of kindness to animals, shelter, food safety and future time. These concepts may form part of themes such as 'Pets', 'Homes', 'Food', and 'When I grow up'. A good time to sing the song is during outside time, when children are building 'hutches' and 'runs' for soft toy rabbits (see below).

Introduce the song by playing the CD and asking everyone to sing along. Let each child make a small 'fly' from black paper and attach it to a short piece of thread. Give each child a soft toy rabbit and ask everyone to sing the song again, as they make their rabbit 'flip and flop' the 'fly' away.

Ask the children to examine their rabbit's nose to see if it's shining and moist, to indicate that the rabbit is healthy.

Talk about how to look after rabbits and arrange for someone to bring a rabbit to visit your setting, if possible. Encourage the children to feel its soft fur (remaining aware of any allergies).

Activity ideas

● Say that wild rabbits live in underground warrens for shelter and rest. Explain that pet rabbits need a hutch and a run. Let everyone use construction bricks to build a hutch and a run for the soft toy rabbits, ideally outside. Give each child a copy of the photocopiable sheet and invite them to draw a rabbit family playing games on the grass. Ask them to draw or stick on pictures of food for them too. **(MD)**

● Tell the children that flies like to crawl in dirty places and that it is not good to let them crawl on our skin or on our food, because they will leave germs. Explain that, especially in summer, we must cover food to protect it from flies. Let one child dangle their 'fly' while another stores replica food safely, using a pretend fridge, food containers and fly covers. **(KUW)**

● Ask if any of the children would like to be a vet when they grow up, talk about what a vet does. Set up a role-play vet's surgery, to care for rabbits in need of treatment. Provide tables and chairs for a waiting room for pet patients and their owners, a large table for the vet to examine animals on and some comfy cushions for the pets to sleep on. Put up posters made by the children about caring for your pet, encouraging the children to include a wide range of different animals. Join the children in acting out caring for the pets. **(CD)**

Little Topsy Rabbit

FUN SONGS for the early years: Animal songs

Little Miss Muffet

**Little Miss Muffet
Sat on her tuffet,**
Children spread out hands, face down, in front of them, and move them slightly in a downward movement, to indicate Miss Muffet's sitting down position.

Eating her curds and whey.
Children mime eating.

**There came a big spider,
Which sat down beside her,**
Children hold up one hand and flutter fingers, moving hand downward, to indicate a spider approaching.

**And frightened Miss Muffet away
And frightened Miss Muffet away.**
Children make a frightened expression, and move fingers on one hand rapidly as they move their arm outwards, to indicate Miss Muffet running away.

Pets

Little Miss Muffet
How to use this song

Learning objectives

Stepping Stone
Express needs and feelings in appropriate ways.

Early Learning Goal
Have a developing awareness of their own needs, views and feelings and be sensitive to the needs, views and feelings of others. **(PSED)**

Group size
Five children.

Props
A plastic spider on a string.

Sharing the song

This rhyme is ideal for developing the concepts of personal change and empathy, the positional concept of 'beside' (as in 'next to') and web formation. Suitable themes are 'All about me', 'Caring and Sharing', 'Spiders' and 'Pattern'. A good time to sing an alternative version of the song (see MD activity below) is as children come to sit at a table. Introduce the song by playing the CD and asking everyone to join in. Ask two children to act out the song, using a plastic spider on a string. Talk about how, in Great Britain, we do not need to be afraid of spiders and how, if they crawl on us, they will only tickle. Sing the song again, substituting the following words for the last line:

And said, 'let's tickle and tickle and play!'

Ask pairs of children to act out the alternative version. Give everyone a copy of the photocopiable sheet and ask them to cut out the spider and attach it to a piece of wool. Make a hole through the black dot on the sheet for them and help them to thread their wool through the hole. Let everyone pull the thread to make the spider tickle Miss Muffet.

Activity ideas

● Encourage the children to talk about how they might once have been a little nervous of certain animals, but no longer are. Ask them what they would say to someone who may still be a little nervous. **(PSED)**

● As children come to sit at a table, one by one, sing the following alternative version of the song, to develop the concept of 'beside':

_____ _____ (child's full name) has sat on his/her chair

To _____ (make a model, for example) right away.

Along comes _____ (next child's name) who sits down beside him/her

And says, 'How are you today?'. Encourage the first child to reply. **(MD)**

● Go on a 'web hunt' and then let everyone make 'webs' by winding silver thread round large pegs in pegboards. **(CD)**

Little Miss Muffet

Farm animals

I Went to Visit a Farm One Day

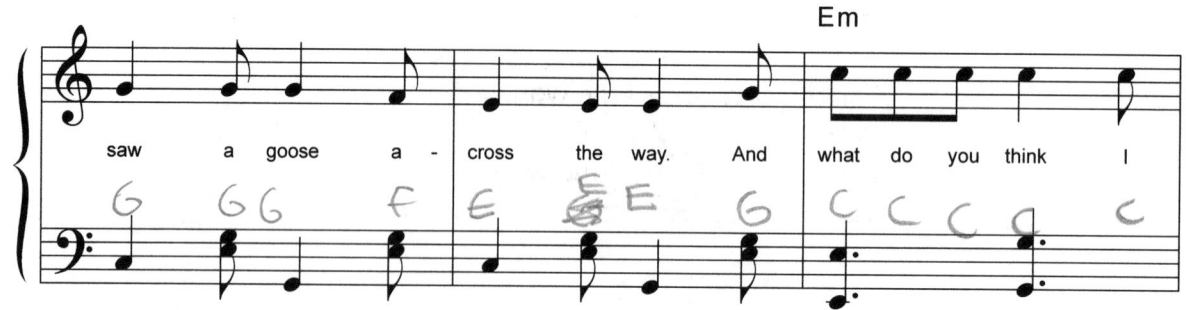

I Went to Visit a Farm One Day

I went to visit a farm one day,
(Children swing arms, as if walking.)

I saw a goose across the way,
(Children put hand above eyes, as if concentrating on what they see.)

And what do you think I heard him say?
(Children put hand to ear.)

'Ssss, ssss, ssss'
(Children make hissing noises.)

Repeat the next two verses, changing animal name and noises.

I saw a cow across the way,
'Moo, moo, moo'
I saw a horse across the way,
'Neigh, neigh, neigh'.

Farm animals

I Went to Visit a Farm One Day
How to use this song

Learning objectives

Stepping Stone
Show interest in illustrations and print in books and print in the environment.

Early Learning Goal
Explore and experiment with sounds, words and texts. **(CLL)**

Group size
Four children, with rest of group watching.

Props
Soft toy or model goose, cow and horse. Large speech bubbles saying 'hiss', 'moo', and 'neigh'.

Sharing the song

This song develops the concept of the printed word as speech written down and the mathematical concepts of a set and counting. It also encourages looking after animals. Appropriate themes are 'Words all around', 'Same and different', 'Farms', and 'People who help us'. The song may be sung whenever the children have completed putting together any animal scene, such as a farm, safari park and so on. Substitute words, as necessary.

Introduce the song by holding up the animals in turn and asking what noises they make. Encourage everyone to sing along to the CD, and make the actions.

Say that we can write animal noises down as words in speech bubbles and show them some examples from magazines. Make some large speech bubbles of your own saying 'hiss', 'moo', and 'neigh'. Ask one child to be the visitor, and three to be animals. As everyone sings, substitute the visitor's name for 'I'. Ask the animals to hold up their speech bubble, making the appropriate noise. Give everyone a copy of the photocopiable sheet and ask them to cut out the speech bubbles and stick them next to the right animal.

Activity ideas

● Encourage the children to adapt the song by singing about other animals and their noises. Ask them to hold up appropriate home-made speech bubbles with the appropriate sounds written in. Ask the children to hold up similar speech bubbles when they sing songs such as 'Old Macdonald had a farm'. Let them make their own animal speech bubbles from card, and attach them to model farm animals with sticky tape or Blu-tack. **(CLL)**

● Let the children sort farm animals into sets, and then count the animals in each set. Encourage the children to sing about the sets, for example, 'I saw nine cows across the way' and make a tape recording of the children singing this numerical version. Give each child a wooden or plastic numeral and ask them to hold it up at the appropriate point in the song when 'their' number is mentioned. **(MD)**

● Invite the children to role-play scenarios involving farmers finding goose eggs, milking cows and managing dray horses. Provide some props to help them do this. **(CD)**

I Went to Visit a Farm One Day

neigh

moo

hiss

Horsey, Horsey

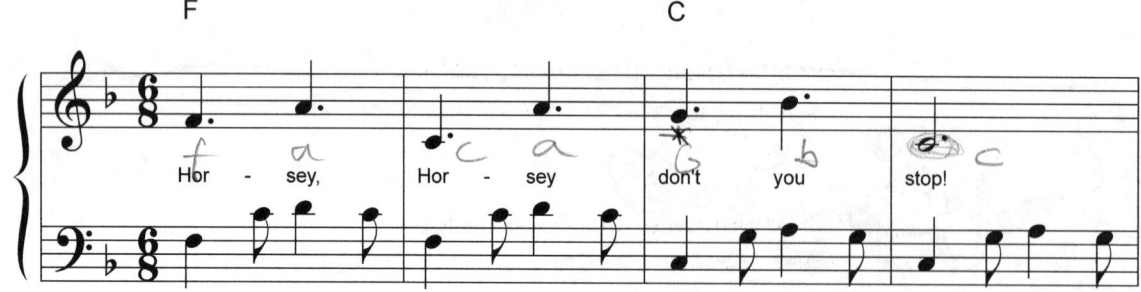

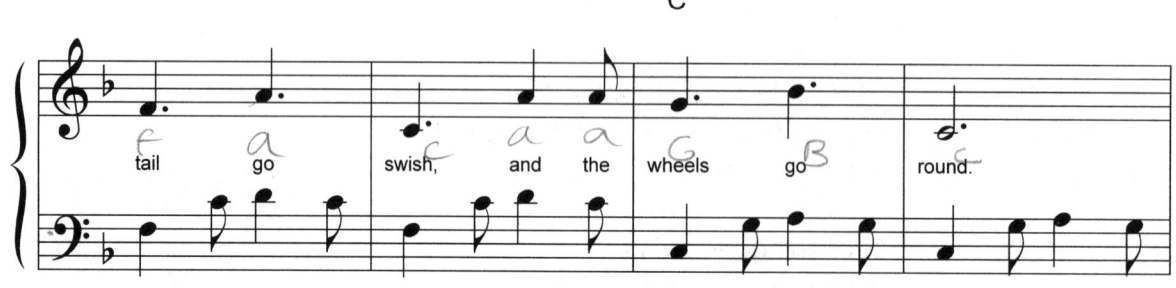

Horsey, Horsey

Horsey, Horsey don't you stop!
(Children wave forefinger from side to side, in a 'no' gesture.)

Just let your feet go clippety-clop
(Children make hands move up and down, by bending their wrists.)

Your tail goes swish,
(Children 'flick' an arm.)

And the wheels go round
(Children make circular hand movements.)

Giddy up!
(Children 'flick' wrist.)

We're homeward bound
(Children point, as if 'homeward'.)

Horsey, Horsey on your way
We've done this journey many a day
(Children nod heads.)

Your tail goes swish
(Children flick an arm.)

And the wheels go round.
(Children make circular hand movements.)

Giddy up!
(Children 'flick' wrist.)

We're homeward bound.
(Children point, as if 'homeward'.)

farm animals

Horsey, Horsey
How to use this song

Learning objectives

Stepping Stone
Show respect for other children's personal space when playing among them.

Early Learning Goal
Show awareness of space, of themselves and others. **(PD)**

Group size
Four children.

Props
Belts.
Thick string.

Sharing the song

This song is valuable for exploring the following concepts: horse-drawn transport, past times, speed, shoeing a horse and the work of blacksmiths. These concepts may be developed in themes such as 'Animals', 'How we used to live', 'Sport' and 'Jobs'. The song is useful to sing when the children are moving from one area of your room to another.

To introduce the song, play the CD. Invite everyone to sing along and to make the appropriate actions. Say that long ago, before cars were invented, people would travel in coaches or carriages pulled by horses and hold up a picture to show them.

Ask the group to get into pairs with one child being the horse and the other the carriage driver. Let the horses wear a belt each, with a short length of thick string (the reins) tied to each side.

Play the song again, with the horses pulling the drivers, who hold the reins. Reverse the roles to give all the children a turn as horse and driver.

Give everyone a copy of the photocopiable sheet, and ask them to draw a driver and reins, and to add circular, card wheels, attached with split pins to the picture of the horse and cart.

Activity ideas

● Talk about and show the children a horseshoe and talk about the work of blacksmiths. Explain that horseshoes make a 'clippety-clop' sound on the ground. Ask one child to be the horse and to put an old, clean pair of children's socks on their hands, and another pair (adult-sized) over their shoes. Ask the child to get down on all fours and put one 'leg' out at a time. The other child, the blacksmith, can gently hammer on four horseshoes, made from card and silver foil, with small balls of Blu-Tack attached. **(KUW)**

● Talk about, and show pictures of, traditional horse-drawn homes, such as Romany caravans (including modern holiday home replicas) and covered wagons. Let children make their own caravans and wagons using a selection of junk materials and dolls' house furniture. **(KUW)**

● Talk about how horses 'trot', 'canter' and 'gallop'. Let children create a course for some horses, using model horses and fences. Ask the children to make their horses trot, canter and gallop around the course. Outside, let children pretend to be horses, moving at the correct speed, as you say 'please trot', and so on. **(PD)**

● Let the children use coconut shells to record the hoof sounds of trotting, cantering and galloping, into a tape recorder. Play the recording back and let everyone pretend to be horses, moving accordingly around the room, varying their speed to suit the different paces. **(CD)**

Horsey, Horsey

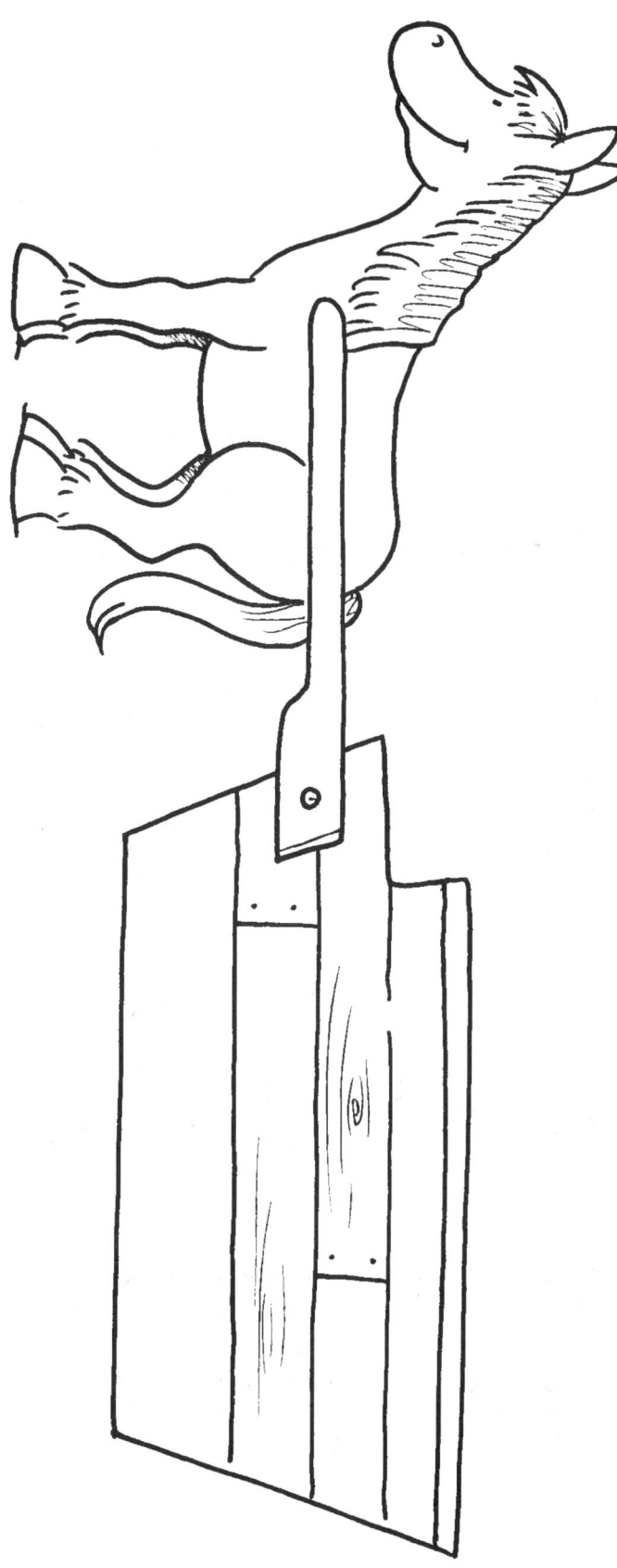

I'm a Duck

Chorus
'Cos I'm a duck
'Quack, quack'
(Children open and close hands in a 'quacking beak' movement.)

I like to go
'Quack, quack.'
'Cos I'm a duck
'Quack, quack'
With feathers on my back
I like to swim all day
(Children move arms in a 'doggy paddle' action.)

And sleep the night away.
(Children put closed hands under cheek and close eyes.)

'Quack, quack'
It's the morning,
Now it's time to play.

Verse 1
When I was a duckling it was fun
Swimming in the lake behind my mum.
But, when I grew big, my mum did say,
(Children lift arms to indicate a large size.)

'Now you are a duck so off you go to play.'
(chorus)

Verse 2
With my big feet I can swim anywhere
Glide across the lake without a care.
(Children make a slow, sweeping movement with arm.)

Underneath the water are things to eat.
(Children point downward.)

When the children throw me bread it really is a treat.
(Children pretend to eat.)
(chorus)

Verse 3
I can flap my wings and fly in the air.
(Children flap arms.)

High up in the sky without a care.
(Children point upwards.)

When I see some water down below
(Children point downwards.)

I land with a splash, start swimming to and fro.
(Children move arms in a 'doggy paddle' action.)

Farm animals

I'm a Duck
How to use this song

Learning objectives

Stepping Stone
Move in a range of ways, such as slithering, shuffling, rolling, crawling, walking, running, jumping, skipping, sliding and hopping.

Early Learning Goal
Move with confidence, imagination and in safety. **(PD)**

Group size
Two children, with any size of group watching.

Props
Duvet, with blue cover or a soft landing mat.

Sharing the song

Use this song to develop the concepts of animal behaviour, empathy, counting and moving through water. Suitable themes are 'Small animals', 'Caring and sharing', 'Let's count' and 'Keep fit'. The song is ideal to sing after telling the story 'The Ugly Duckling'.

To introduce the song, ask everyone to sing along to the CD and make the actions. Ask two children (with their shoes removed) to be a mother duck and her duckling. Use an old duvet (covered in blue material) or a soft landing mat to represent the duck pond.

Ask the mother duck to teach her duckling how to swim on the 'pond', and ask the duckling to demonstrate gliding and diving, as everyone sings the song again.

Give everyone a copy of the photocopiable sheet and ask them to cut out the mother duck and the duckling and to attach a short piece of straw to the top of them both. Ask the children to manoeuvre them around (one in each hand), as the mother teaches her duckling how to swim, splash and glide.

Activity ideas

● Sing the song from 'The Ugly Duckling' (Traditional) ('There once was an ugly duckling...') and ask everyone to say how the duckling felt when his sisters and brothers were unkind to him because he looked different from them. Talk about how it is wrong to hurt somebody's feelings because they do not look the same. Explain that although people may look different on the outside, people have the same feelings on the inside and they can be hurt by unkind words. **(PSED)**

● Play a counting game 'Feed the duck in the park' by inviting one child to be the duck on a pond in a park (blue-covered duvet, blue plastic cloth or a hoop). Ask the duck to say 'quack' a number of times, to indicate how many bread cubes they would like a visiting child to gently throw onto the pond for them. **(MD)**

● Talk about a duck's webbed feet and look at pictures in books. Explain that the 'webs' help the duck to push water and swim well. Examine a pair of swimming flippers together and talk about how they help a swimmer. **(KUW)**

I'm a Duck

Hey, Diddle Diddle

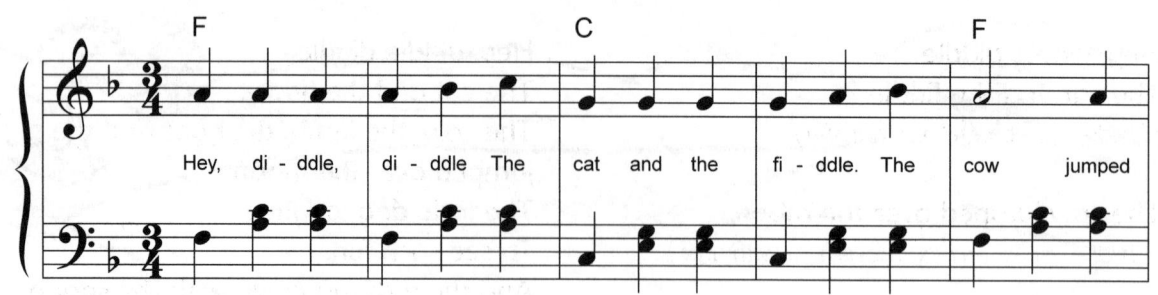

Hey, Diddle Diddle

Hey, diddle diddle
The cat and the fiddle.
(Children pretend to play a fiddle.)

The cow jumped over the moon.
(Children make arching movement with arm.)

The little dog laughed to see such fun.
And the dish ran away with the spoon.
(Children move index and third finger quickly, to indicate 'running'.)

Hey, diddle diddle
The cat and the fiddle.
(Repeat actions as above for all verses.)

The cow and the lamb jumped over the moon.
The little dog laughed
To see such fun.
And the dish ran away with the spoon.

Hey, diddle diddle
The cat and the fiddle.
The cow, the lamb and the goat jumped over the moon.
The little dog laughed
To see such fun.
And the dish ran away with the spoon.

Hey, diddle diddle
The cat and the fiddle.
The cow, the lamb, the goat and the pig jumped over the moon.
The little dog laughed
To see such fun.
And the dish ran away with the spoon.

Hey, diddle diddle
The cat and the fiddle.
The cow, the lamb, the goat, the pig and the horse jumped over the moon.
The little dog howled
At what came next...
Then he too jumped over the moon.
(Last line of song.)

Well, wouldn't you?
(Children spread out both arms, palms upwards, and smile, to invite agreement.)

FUN SONGS for the early years: Animal songs

Farm animals

Hey, Diddle Diddle
How to use this song

Learning objectives

Stepping Stone
Use some number names and number language spontaneously.

Early Learning Goal
Say and use number names in order in familiar contexts. **(MD)**

Group size
Six children, with any size of group watching.

Props
A crescent moon made from a piece of card covered in silver foil, stuck to the side of a shoe box.

Sharing the song

Use this song to explore the concepts related to ordinal number, musical instruments, kitchen utensils, counting items that cannot be touched, rhymes, phases of the moon and festival symbols. Incorporate the song in themes such as 'Number games', 'Music', 'Cooking', 'Rhyme time', 'The sky', and 'Eid-ul-Fitr'. A good time to sing it is when the children are being called one at a time to a different area, for example, when the children are asked to put on their coats they can jump over the moon (see Props) on the way.

Invite everyone to join in with the CD. Let a group of six children choose which animals to be. Ask everyone to sing again, as each child jumps over the card moon when they are referred to in the song. Encourage them to use finger puppets made from the photocopiable sheet and make them 'jump' over the moon on the sheet, as they sing.

Activity ideas

● Encourage the children to substitute the names of other musical instruments and kitchen utensils for fun, for example 'Hey, diddle diddle the cat and the trumpet' and 'The dish ran away with the fork'. Talk about pairs of words that rhyme and do not rhyme. **(CLL)**

● Collect pairs of items, such as a knife and fork, cup and saucer, bat and ball. Put one item from each pair in a drawstring bag. Invite indivual children to remove an item and name its partner. Next, ask them to recite the rhyme, substituting the new pair of items in place of dish and spoon. Discuss which one makes the most sense! **(CLL)**

● Place the shoebox moon on a table and ask one child to turn their back to the group. Ask another child to put a number of model animals (up to four) on a plate, and then make them 'jump over the moon' one at a time. Invite a third child to play a drum beat each time an animal jumps. Ask the first child to count the drumbeats and say how many animals jumped. **(MD)**

● Explain very simply the phases of the moon and what a crescent moon looks like (show the card moon attached to a shoebox). Say that on the cards that Muslim people send to one another for the festival of Eid-ul-Fitr (celebrated in November each year), there is a crescent moon. This is because Muslim people must look in the sky to see a crescent moon to know that the month of Ramadan has finished, and that the festival of Eid-ul-Fitr can begin. **(KUW)**

● Let the children investigate other ways of moving, in addition to jumping over the moon. Challenge them to show you how they can step, hop and skip over the moon. **(PD)**

Hey, Diddle Diddle

# Farm animals

Two Little Chickens

Two little chickens looking for some more. A-

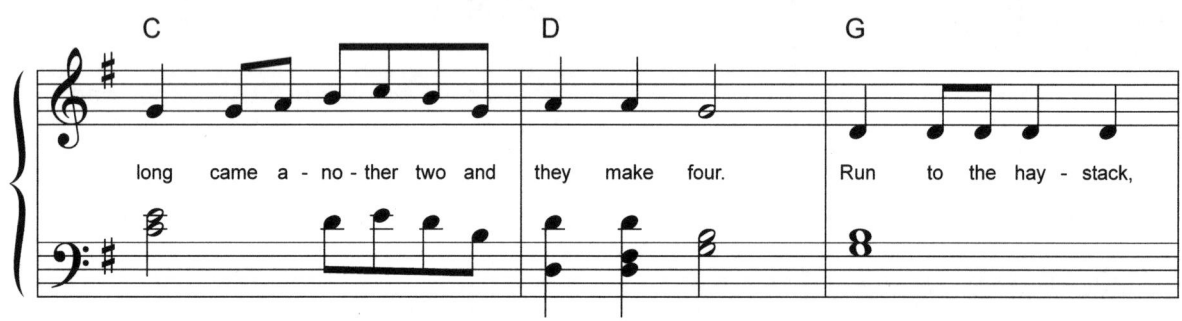

long came a-nother two and they make four. Run to the hay-stack,

run to the pen. Run little chickens, back to mo-ther hen.

Two Little Chickens

Two little chickens looking for some more.
(Children wiggle two fingers.)

Along came another two and they make four.
(Children wiggle four fingers.)

Run to the haystack, run to the pen.
(Children make running movements with four fingers.)

Run little chickens, back to mother hen.
(Children open arms out wide in a welcoming gesture.)

Four little chickens getting in a fix.
(Children wiggle four fingers.)

Along came another two and they make six.
(Children wiggle six fingers.)

Run to the haystack, run to the pen.
(Children make running movements with six fingers.)

Run little chickens, back to mother hen.
(Children open arms out wide.)

Six little chickens perching on a gate.
(Children hold up six fingers and keep them still.)

Along came another two and they make eight.
(Children hold up eight fingers and keep them still.)

Run to the haystack, run to the pen.
(Children make running movements with eight fingers.)

Run little chickens, back to mother hen.
(Children open arms out wide.)

Eight little chickens run to mother hen.
(Children make running movements with eight fingers.)

Along came another two and they make ten.
(Children make running movements with 10 fingers.)

Run to the haystack, run to the pen.
(Children make running movements with 10 fingers.)

Run little chickens, back to mother hen.
(Children open arms out wide.)

farm animals

Two Little Chickens
How to use this song

Learning objectives

Stepping Stone
Find the total number of items in two groups by counting all of them.

Early Learning Goal
Begin to relate addition to combining two groups of objects, and subtraction to 'taking away'. **(MD)**

Group size
Eleven children.

Props
A 'chicken abacus' (see illustration).

Sharing the song

The song covers the concepts of addition, farm work and cooking with eggs. The song may form part of themes such as 'Let's count', 'On the farm' and 'Food'. Link the song with the story of 'The Little Red Hen' (Traditional) and say that the song is about the Little Red Hen's chicks. Introduce the song by inviting everyone to join in with the CD. Make a chicken abacus following the illustrations right. Stick drawings of chickens onto lengths of kitchen roll tubes and thread a length of thick string through them. Attach it to two chairs. Invite children to slide the chickens along the abacus in answer to your addition questions.

Activity ideas

● Invite the children to make a 'chicken run' each on a table, using toothpaste tube boxes for the walls and a small food packet for the hen pen. Alternatively, use small bricks. Give each child ten yellow cotton wool balls to represent chickens, and talk through addition scenarios with them. **(MD)**

● Talk about how farmers collect mother hens' eggs from hen pens, and how eggs can be used in different recipes. Make a group book called 'We love eggs', with drawings of children eating poached, scrambled and boiled eggs, pancakes and omelettes. Try some egg recipes together. **(KUW)**

● Explain what a 'haystack' is and sing the traditional nursery rhyme 'Little Boy Blue'. Talk about the work of shepherds and chicken farmers, who both ensure their animals do not get lost. Say that Little Boy Blue sometimes had to look after chickens, as well as sheep. Change the

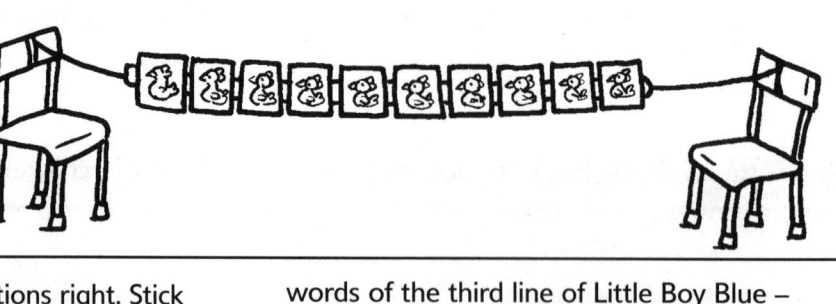

words of the third line of Little Boy Blue – 'The sheep are in the meadow' – to 'The chicks are in the chicken run'. Ask one child (Little Boy Blue) to pretend to sleep 'under the haystack' (yellow material covering a table). Ask Little Boy Blue to wake up and call out a number, to indicate how many children (chickens) at a time should run to the haystack, the pen (made from bricks) and, finally, to mother hen. Organise the other children to respond to the instructions. **(CD)**

Two Little Chickens

4   8   6   10

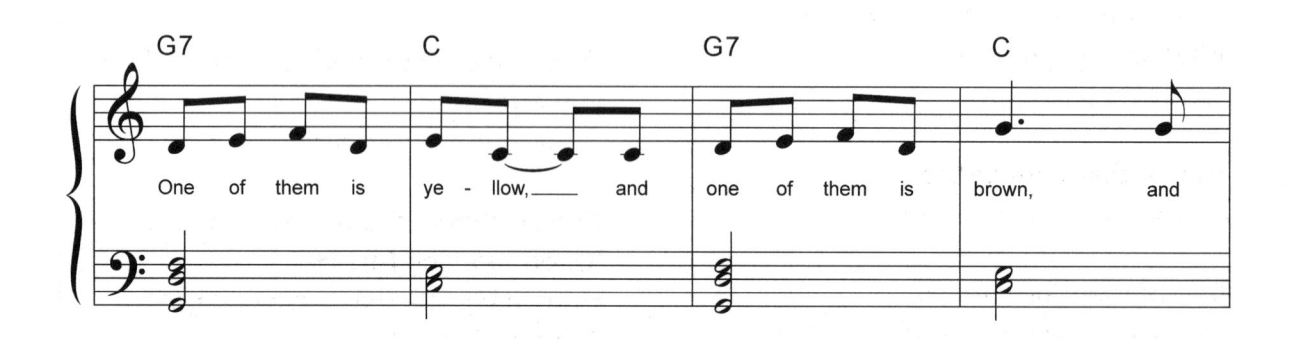

Chook, Chook

Chook, chook, chook, chook, chook. 'Good morn-ing Mrs Hen'.

'How ma-ny chi-ckens have you got?' 'Ma-dam I've got ten.

One of them is ye-llow, and one of them is brown, and

eight of them are spe-ckled but the fi-nest in the town'.

Chook, Chook

Chook, chook, chook, chook, chook
'Good morning Mrs Hen.
'How many chickens have you got?'
'Madam I've got ten.
(Children hold up ten fingers.)

One of them is yellow
(Children hold up one finger.)

And one of them is brown
(Children hold up one finger.)

And eight of them are speckled but the finest in the town.'
(Children hold up eight fingers.)

Chook, chook, chook, chook, chook
'Good morning Mrs Hen.
How many chickens have you got?'
'Madam I've got ten.
(Children hold up ten fingers.)

Two of them are yellow
(Children hold up two fingers.)

Two of them are brown
(Children hold up two fingers.)

Six of them are speckled but the finest in the town.'
(Children hold up six fingers.)

Chook, chook, chook, chook, chook
'Good morning Mrs Hen.
How many chickens have you got?'
'Madam I've got ten.
(Children hold up ten fingers.)

Three of them are yellow
(Children hold up three fingers.)

Three of them are brown
(Children hold up three fingers.)

Four of them are speckled but the finest in the town.'
(Children hold up four fingers)

Chook, chook, chook, chook, chook
'Good morning Mrs Hen.
How many chickens have you got?'
'Madam I've got ten.
(Children hold up ten fingers.)

Four of them are yellow
(Children hold up four fingers.)

Four of them are brown
(Children hold up four fingers.)

Two of them are speckled but the finest in the town.'
(Children hold up two fingers.)

Chook, chook, chook, chook, chook
'Good morning Mrs Hen.
How many chickens have you got?'
'Madam I've got ten.
(Children hold up ten fingers.)

Five of them are yellow
(Children hold up five fingers.)

Five of them are brown
(Children hold up five fingers.)

None of them are speckled but the finest in the town.'
(Children hold up two 'fists', to indicate no speckled eggs.)

Farm animals

Chook, Chook
How to use this song

Learning objectives

Stepping Stone
Count up to three or four objects by saying one number name for each item.

Early Learning Goal
Count reliably up to 10 everyday objects. **(MD)**

Group size
Five children.

Sharing the song

This song is useful for developing concepts of counting and addition, politeness, poultry breeds and the meaning of the word 'speckled'. These concepts may be explored in themes such as 'Let's count', 'Caring and sharing', 'Farm animals' and 'Pattern'.

The first three lines of the song are ideal for use at circle time: ask the children in the circle to be Mrs Hens, choose one child to be a customer. The customer stands in the centre and asks one of the Mrs Hens how many chickens she has. Mrs Hen should then say a number and hold up the right number of fingers to indicate how many.

Introduce the song by asking everyone to sing along to the CD.

Give each child a copy of the photocopiable sheet and a yellow and a brown crayon. Ask everyone to sing the song again, one verse at a time. Between verses, ask the children to add yellow, brown and 'speckled' dots to the chickens in one row at a time, according to the words in each verse.

Activity ideas

● Talk about the terms 'madam' and 'sir'. Ask Mrs Hen to use the terms correctly, according to whether she is replying to a girl or boy customer. Sing the traditional nursery rhyme 'Baa Baa Black Sheep', and ask everyone to sing 'Yes sir, yes sir', or 'Yes madam, yes madam', according to whether the questioner is a boy or girl. Show the children examples of letters, beginning 'Dear Sir' or 'Dear Madam'. Say that shop assistants sometimes call customers 'sir' or 'madam'. Encourage children to say 'May I help you, sir (madam)?' in their role-play. **(CLL)**

● Talk about the title of the song and how this is the sound the hens make. Ask the children to think about the sounds that other animals make and to copy them. **(CLL)**

● Give four children a hundred-peg board each. Ask them to place one yellow and one brown peg at the beginning of a row. Then ask them to choose another colour peg and to complete the row with this third colour. Say to one child 'How many pegs have you got?' Encourage the reply 'I've got ten. One of them is yellow, one of them is brown and eight of them are (for example) green'. Continue with different combinations of ten as in the song. **(MD)**

● Encourage the children to find out about different breeds of hen and cocks, and their feathers. Use animal reference books and ask the children to look carefully at model poultry and pictures in farm story books, and say what breed they think the hens and cocks are. **(KUW)**

● Talk about the meaning of the word 'speckled'. If possible, show examples of speckled eggs and pottery, such as vases and crockery. Say that some people's skin looks speckled with freckles. Sing the song 'Five little speckled frogs', and let the children experiment with splatter painting, to produce speckled effects. **(CD)**

Chook Chook

Farm animals

Fieldmice

Down in the meadow where the long grass grows. There were five little field mice washing their clothes. With a rub-a-dub here and a rub-a-dub there. That's the way the field-mice wash their clothes. With a squeak, squeak, squeak boogy-woogy. Squeak, squeak, squeak boogy-woogy. Squeak, squeak, squeak boogy woogy. That's the way the field-mice wash their clothes.

Farm animals

Fieldmice

Down in the meadow where the long grass grows
(Children lift arms and wave them around, like long grass swaying.)

There were five little field mice washing their clothes.
(Children hold up five fingers.)

With rub-a-dub here and a rub-a-dub there,
(Children make 'scrubbing' movements.)

That's the way the fieldmice wash their clothes.
With a squeak, squeak, squeak boogy-woogy.
(Children 'squeak' and shake their heads and shoulders.)

Squeak, squeak, squeak boogy-woogy.
Squeak, squeak, squeak boogy-woogy.
That's the way the fieldmice wash their clothes.
(Count down: four, three, two.)

There was one little fieldmouse washing his clothes

FUN SONGS for the early years: Animal songs

Farm animals

Fieldmice
How to use this song

Learning objectives

Stepping Stone
Describe simple features of objects and events.

Early Learning Goal
Find out about and identify some features of living things, objects and events they observe. **(KUW)**

Group size
Five children.

Props
Ten items of dolls' clothing, five slightly muddied.
Water in water tray.
Blue material (a river).
Five pebbles.

Sharing the song

Use this song to develop concepts of subtraction, personal safety, times past, and evaporation, in themes such as 'How many?', 'Keeping safe', 'Long ago' and 'Weather'. A good time to sing it is when the children are outside: play the song on a CD player in battery mode, as children (the fieldmice) wash their clothes in a river.

As an introduction, ask everyone to sing with the CD. Give everyone a slightly muddied doll's garment to wash without soap. Say that the fieldmice would not have had soap products, only stones to rub away dirt, as people did long ago. Ask everyone to kneel behind blue material (a river) with a clean garment and a pebble each, and to sing again, as they scrub. As each fieldmouse leaves, ask how many are left.

Give everyone a copy of the photocopiable sheet and ask them to draw one garment in the river for each fieldmouse.

Activity ideas

● Talk about keeping safe near water, in the home, and outside. Talk about the dangers of water. Make a large book, called 'Safe water fun!'. Ask children to draw pictures and to cut out catalogue pictures of baths, paddling pools and so on. Ask them to stick in the pictures, adding hand-drawn children. Encourage everyone to write or dictate comments about keeping safe. **(PSED)**

● Ask children to hold up five fingers, and to work out subtraction problems based on the song, for example, 'There were five fieldmice washing their clothes. Two finished and went away. How many were left?' Ask two children to hold up a skipping rope (washing line), ask a third child to place some dolls' clothes on the line and to count them. Ask the rest of the group to make the sound of wind blowing, and the third child to gently push one garment off the line. Ask how many are left. **(MD)**

● Say that the fieldmice did not have tumble dryers. Rig up a small clothes line outside to dry the dolls' clothes used in the 'Sharing the song' activity (see above). Explain that the water in the clothes evaporates. **(KUW)**

FUN SONGS for the early years: Animal songs

Fieldmice

farm animals

Two Little Dicky Birds

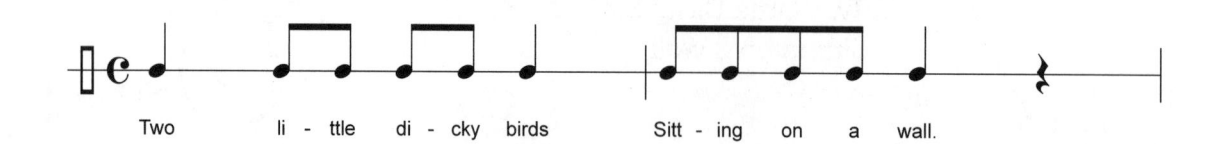

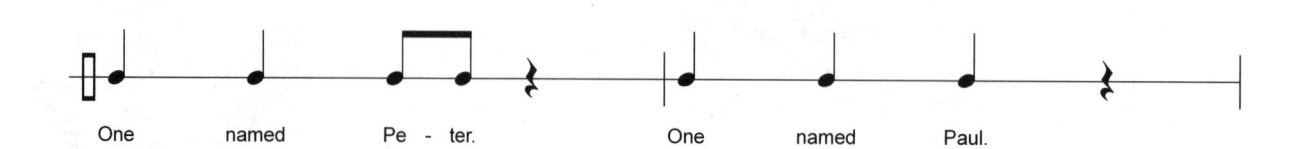

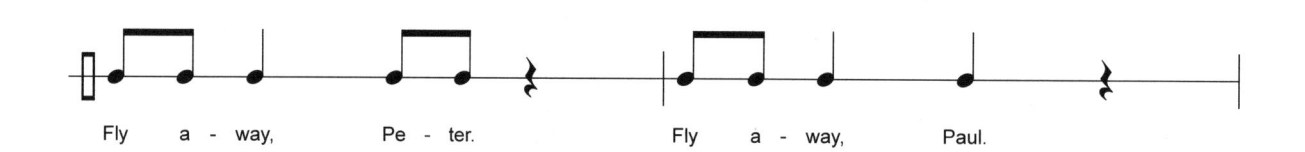

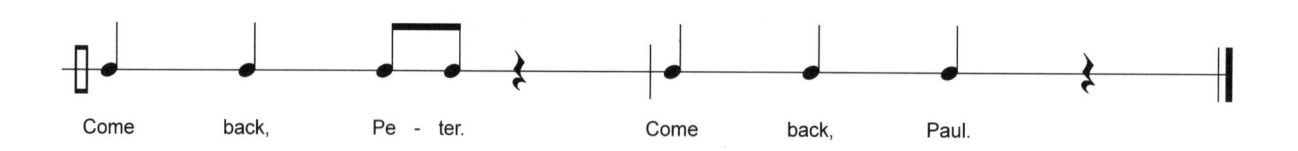

Two li-ttle di-cky birds Sitt-ing on a wall.

One named Pe-ter. One named Paul.

Fly a-way, Pe-ter. Fly a-way, Paul.

Come back, Pe-ter. Come back, Paul.

Two Little Dicky Birds

Two Little Dicky Birds
Sitting on a wall.
(Children put up two fingers.)

One named Peter,
One named Paul.
Fly away, Peter.
(Children make arc with their arm and bring it back and put one finger up, to show that only Paul is left.)

Fly away, Paul.
(Children make arc with arm, bring it back and show a fist (no fingers) to show that no birds are left.)

Come back, Peter.
(Children make an arc with arm, bring it back and put one finger up, to show that Peter has flown back.)

Come back, Paul.
(Children make an arc with arm, bring it back and put another finger up, to show that Paul has also flown back.)

(repeat x 2)
Come back, Peter.
Come back, Paul.
Come back, Peter.
Come back, Paul.
Come back, Peter.
Come back, Paul.

farm animals

Two Little Dicky Birds
How to use this song

Learning objectives

Stepping Stone
Hear and say the initial sounds in words and know which letters represent some of the sounds.

Early Learning Goal
Hear and say initial and final sounds in words and short vowel sounds within words. **(CLL)**

Group size
Six children.

Sharing the song

This song incorporates concepts of initial letter sounds, subtraction, kindness to animals, and seasons. Include the song in themes such as 'Let's listen', 'Counting games', 'Gardens' and 'Seasons'. Sing the first verse at home time, substituting the children's names and singing 'Goodbye' instead of 'Fly away', and 'See you soon' instead of 'Come back'. By way of introduction, ask the group to sing along to the CD. Say that the names 'Peter' and 'Paul' begin with the same sound.

Ask for the names of children in your setting who share the same initial letter sound in their first name. Sing the song again, substituting these names for 'Peter' and 'Paul'.

Give everyone a copy of the photocopiable sheet and ask them to write in the initial capital letters, pointing out the matching pairs. If the children cannot copy the letters, ask them to draw a line instead, or provide dotted guidelines for them to follow.

Activity ideas

● Talk about being kind to all animals, including birds. Ask the children for ideas of how to be kind. Encourage suggestions such as putting out food in winter time (see activity below), providing bird tables, not disturbing birds' nests, taking injured birds to a vet, and knowing about and visiting bird sanctuaries. **(PSED)**

● Help each child, as necessary, to make a simple 'twirling' picture, using a split pin, to use when they sing the song, to show that 'if there are two birds and one flies away, there will be one left, but if that bird flies away too, there will be no birds left, until they both fly back again!' (see illustration below). **(MD)**

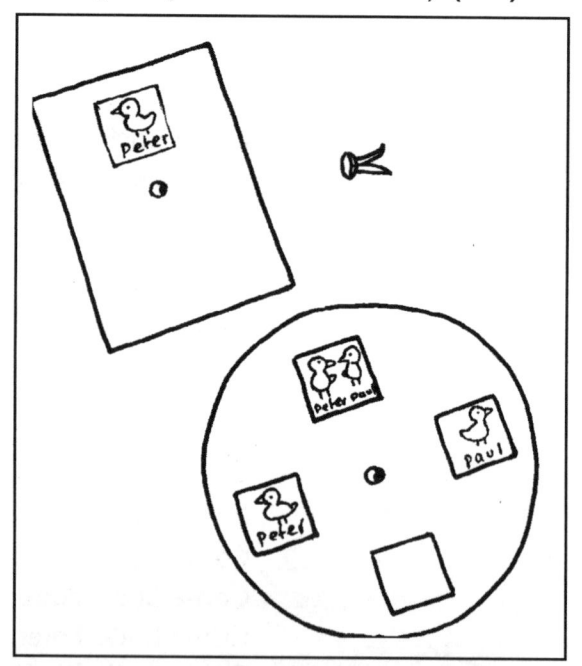

● Make a winter bird cake: make two holes in a margarine tub, just under the rim, using an awl – a pointed hand tool for piercing tough materials. Melt half a block of vegetable fat and, while it is still soft and only warm, transfer to a dish. Let everyone mix in scraps of cheese, fruit and crumbs. (Do not use nuts because of the danger of choking or allergic reaction in children.) Pour the mixture into the tub, press down firmly and leave to solidify. Thread string through the holes and hang in the garden. **(KUW)**

Two Little Dicky Birds

_ax

_egan

_oe

_essica

_ulemain

_arah

| S S | M M | J J |

Wild animals

Down in the Jungle

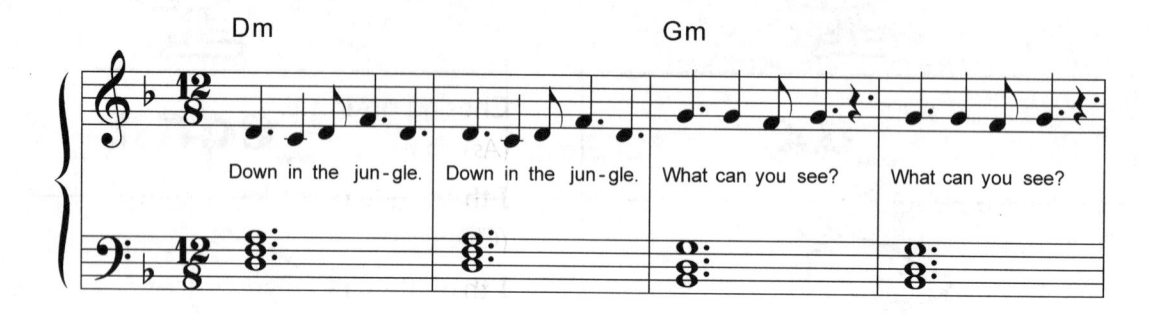

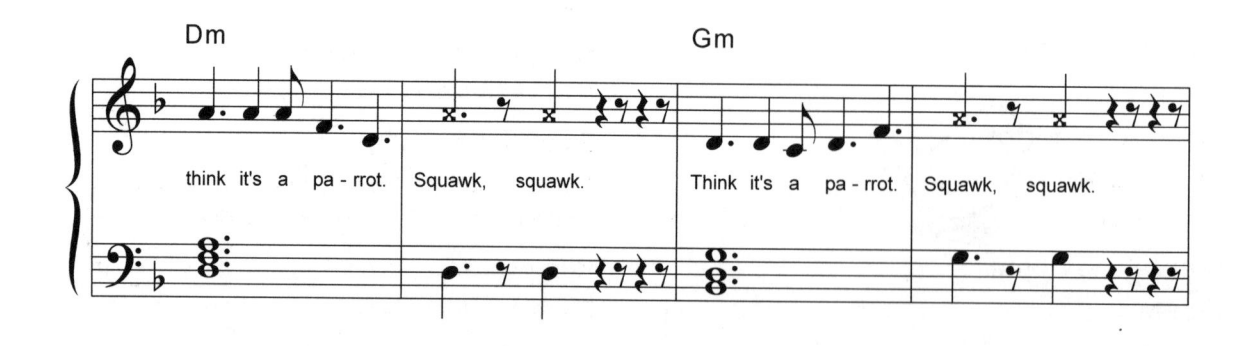

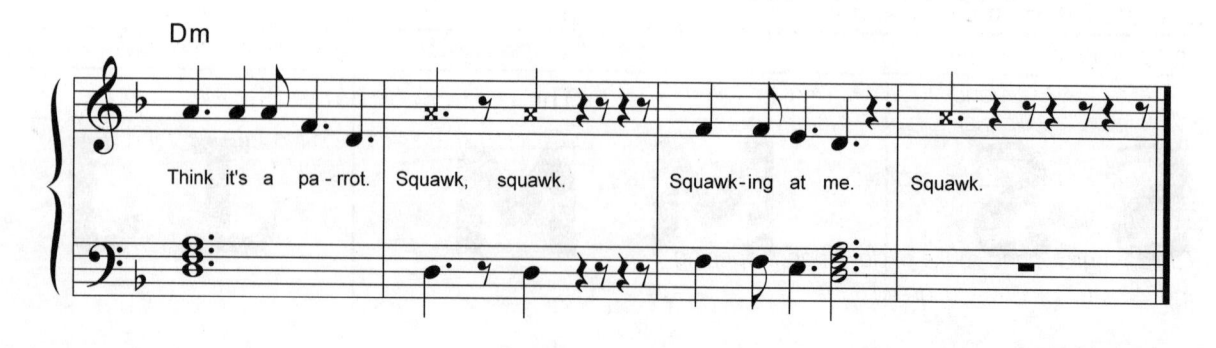

Down in the jungle. Down in the jungle. What can you see? What can you see?

I can hear a noise. I can hear a noise. What can it be? What can it be? Well I

think it's a parrot. Squawk, squawk. Think it's a parrot. Squawk, squawk.

Think it's a parrot. Squawk, squawk. Squawk-ing at me. Squawk.

Down in the Jungle

Down in the jungle,
Down in the jungle.
What can you see?
(Children put hand above their eyes, to shut out sun's glare, so that they can see properly.)

What can you see?
(As above.)

I can hear a noise,
(Children put hand to ear.)

I can hear a noise.
(As above.)

What can it be?
(Children spread out both hands in a 'questioning' gesture.)

What can it be?
(As above.)

Well, I think it's a parrot.
Squawk, squawk.
(Children 'squawk' and move their hand to resemble a parrot's beak opening and closing.)

Think it's a parrot.
Squawk, squawk.
(As above.)

Think it's a parrot.
Squawk, squawk.
(As above.)

Squawking at me.
Squawk.
(As above.)

2. Well, I think it's a crocodile
Snap, snap.
(Children put two hands together, to resemble a crocodile's mouth opening and closing.)

3. Well, I think it's a tiger.
Growl, growl.
(Children growl and make a 'claw' hand, opening and closing, to convey a 'growl'.)

Want to go home now.
Want to go home now.
Chasing after me.
(Children make fingers move in a rapid 'running' motion.)

Chasing after me.
(As above.)

I think they're feeling hungry.
(Children rub tummies.)

I think they're feeling hungry.
(As above.)

It's time for their tea.
(Children look at their wrists, as if looking at their watches, to check that it's tea time.)

It's time for their tea.
(As above.)

Run past the tiger
(Children rotate elbows, as if running.)

Growl, growl.
(Children growl and make a 'claw' hand, opening and closing, to convey a 'growl'.)

Run past the crocodile
(Children rotate elbows, as if running.)

Snap, snap.
(Children put two hands together, to resemble a crocodile's mouth opening and closing.)

Run past the parrot
(Children rotate elbows, as if running.)

Squawk, squawk.
(Children 'squawk' and move their hand, to resemble a parrot's beak opening and closing.)

They didn't catch me! Phew!
(Children shake heads to indicate 'no', and blow a sigh of relief.)

Wild animals

Down in the Jungle
How to use this song

Learning objectives

Stepping Stone
Try to capture experiences and responses with music, dance, paint and other materials or words.

Early Learning Goal
Express and communicate their ideas, thoughts and feelings by using a widening range of materials, suitable tools, imaginative and role-play, movement, designing and making, and a variety of songs and musical instruments. **(CD)**

Group size
Four children.

Props
Animal masks and outfits.
Scarves in appropriate colours and patterns.
Green material for foliage.

Sharing the song

Use this song to help the children understand the concept of animals in the wild, giving directions, instructing a programmable toy and jungle life. Include the song when planning themes such as 'Wild animals', 'People who help us', 'Technology all around' and 'All around the world'. The song works very well outside, when played on a CD player in battery mode.

Let one child 'tread carefully through the jungle', while the other children pretend to be the animals. Invite everyone to join in with the CD, and suggest what the children can put on to dress up as the jungle animals, what they can use to make the animal noises and also ideas for jungle 'foliage'.

Encourage the group to sing again, while acting out the scenario.

Activity ideas

● Invite the children to create a jungle area on a green plastic cloth on the floor using model animals and play people. Stick small lengths of real or plastic greenery in Blu-tak on upturned lids, for foliage. (Check that any real greenery used is non-poisonous). Use arrangements of distinctive stones as landmarks. Let the children place animals in groups in the jungle and use play people as safari guides to give directions to other play people (travellers) who want to see certain animals. Give each child a copy of the photocopiable sheet and ask them to cut out and stick on the groups of animals wherever they wish and to draw a line to show their route as an explorer. Ask them to describe the animals' actions. **(CLL)**

● When a group has arranged a variety of animals in a 'jungle', give one child a pair of binoculars or a telescope. Ask them to focus on one animal, without telling anyone what it is. Ask them to describe its appearance or position, for others to guess which animal they are looking at. **(CLL)**

● Encourage the children to create a safari park. Stick a small tour bus on top of a Roamer or a remote-controlled vehicle with Blu-tack. Ask individual children to act as a bus driver to take the visitors in the tour bus to see certain animals. **(KUW)**

● Let children create a damp jungle in damp sand (inside or outside), using twigs, leaves, small branches, stones and 'swamps' and 'lakes' made from aluminium foil food containers, filled with mud or water, 'waterfalls' made with large stones. Encourage them to use model animals and play people to explore the environment. **(CD)**

Down in the Jungle

Wild animals

Nellie the Elephant

Words by Ralph Butler, Music by Peter Hart. Published by Dash Music.

To Bombay A travelling circus came. They brought an intelligent elephant, And Nellie was her name. One dark night, She slipped her iron chain. And off she went to Hindustan and was never seen again. Nellie the Elephant packed her trunk and said goodbye to the circus. Off she went with a trumpety-trump, Trump, trump, trump. Nellie the Elephant packed her trunk and trundled back to the jungle. Off she went with a trumpety-trump, Trump, trump, trump. The head of the herd was calling Far, far away. They met one night in the silver light on the road to Mandalay. Nellie the Elephant packed her trunk and said goodbye to the circus. Off she went with a trumpety-trump, Trump, trump, trump.

Nellie the Elephant

Words by Ralph Butler, Music by Peter Hart. Published by Dash Music.

To Bombay, A travelling circus came.
They brought an intelligent elephant,
(Children wave an arm in front of their nose.)
And Nellie was her name.
One dark night,
She slipped her iron chain.
(Children lift a leg, to indicate Nellie escaping.)
And off she ran to Hindustan
(Children move fingers rapidly, to convey 'running'.)
And was never seen again.
(Children shake heads and wave index finger, to convey 'never'.)
Nellie the elephant packed her trunk
(Children mime packing a suitcase.)
And said goodbye to the circus.
(Children wave 'goodbye'.)
Off she went with a trumpety-trump,
(Children lift arm in air, as if 'trumpeting' like an elephant.)
Trump, trump, trump.
Nellie the elephant packed her trunk
(Children mime packing a suitcase.)
And trundled back to the jungle.
Off she went with a trumpety-trump,
(Children lift arm in air, as if 'trumpeting' like an elephant.)
Trump, trump, trump.
The head of the herd was calling
(Children touch ear, as if listening.)
Far, far away.
They met one night in the silver light
On the road to Mandalay.
Nellie the elephant packed her trunk
(Children mime packing a suitcase.)
And said goodbye to the circus.
(Children wave goodbye.)
Off she went with a trumpety-trump,
(Children lift arm in air, as if 'trumpeting' like an elephant.)
Trump, trump, trump.

Night by night,
She danced with the circus band.
(Children point index finger downwards and make circular motion, to convey idea of Nellie twirling around, as she danced.)
When Nellie was leading the big parade
She looked so proud and grand.
(Children lift heads in the air, 'proudly'.)
No more tricks, For Nellie to perform.
They taught her how to take a bow
(Children bow.)
She took the crowd by storm.
Nellie the elephant packed her trunk
(Children mime packing a suitcase.)
And said goodbye to the circus.
(Children wave goodbye.)
Off she went with a trumpety-trump,
(Children lift arm in the air, as if 'trumpeting' like an elephant.)
Trump, trump, trump.
Nellie the elephant packed her trunk
(Children mime packing a suitcase.)
And trundled back to the jungle.
Off she went with a trumpety-trump,
(Children lift arm in the air, as if 'trumpeting' like an elephant.)
Trump, trump, trump.
The head of the herd was calling
Far, far away.
They met one night in the silver light
On the road to Mandalay.
Nellie the elephant packed her trunk
(Children mime packing a suitcase.)
And said goodbye to the circus.
(Children wave goodbye.)
Off she went with a trumpety-trump,
(Children lift arm in the air, as if 'trumpeting' like an elephant.)
Trump, trump, trump.
Trump, trump, trump.

Wild animals

Nellie the Elephant
How to use this song

Learning objectives

Stepping Stone
Listen to favourite nursery rhymes, stories and songs. Join in with repeated refrains, anticipating key events and important phrases.

Early Learning Goal
Listen with enjoyment, and respond to stories, songs and other music, rhymes and poems and make up their own stories, songs, rhymes and poems. **(CLL)**

Group size
Six children.

Props
A3 copy of the photocopiable sheet.
Four pegs.
Thick string.

Sharing the song

The song can be used to develop the concepts of continuing a story, kindness to animals, and elephant behaviour. Suitable themes are 'Story fun', 'Caring and sharing', and 'Large animals'. A good time to sing the song is when the children are playing with model elephants. You may prefer to enlarge the music on page 54.

Before introducing the song, cut out the four pictures from the enlarged photocopiable sheet and peg them to a suspended length of thick string. Play the song, inviting everyone to join in. Talk through the pictures. Suggest that when Nellie got back to the jungle, her family and friends gave her a party. Ask for ideas about what the elephants would have done at the party.

Give everyone a copy of the photocopiable sheet and ask them to act out the pictures and then to arrange them in the right order, sticking them in place when they are happy with the order.

Activity ideas

● Talk about how animals used to perform in circuses but that we now think this is unkind. Ask whether anyone has visited a circus, and what they saw. Put chairs in a circle, and enact your own circus, with children demonstrating circus skills such as walking on a tightrope using a skipping rope on the floor, jumping through a hoop, balancing a beanbag on parts of the body and having clown fun. **(PSED)**

● Explain that when elephants drink, they suck water up their trunk and then squirt it into their mouth. Let everyone make an 'elephant straw', to show how elephants suck up water. Let each child draw an elephant's face on card and cut it out. Make a hole between the eyes, and help each child, as necessary, to push a wide, 'bendy' straw through the hole, to become the elephant's 'trunk' (see illustration below). **(KUW)**

● Invite the children to move around like elephants, using their hands as big ears and flapping them to get rid of flies, bathing, spraying themselves with dust to keep cool, lifting things with their trunks. **(PD)**

Nellie the Elephant

Wild animals

When Goldilocks Went to the House of the Bears

When Gol-di-locks went to the house of the bears Oh what did her blue eyes see? A bowl that was huge, a bowl that was small and a bowl that was ti-ny and that's not all. She coun-ted them one, two, three.

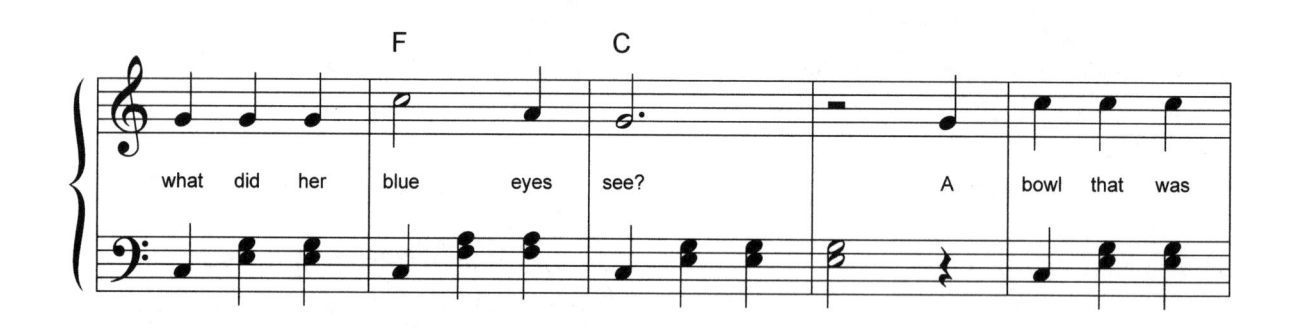

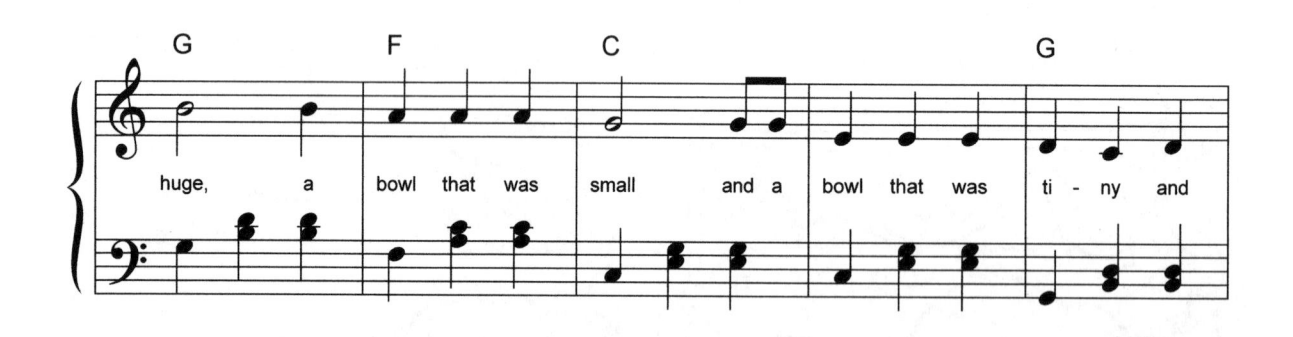

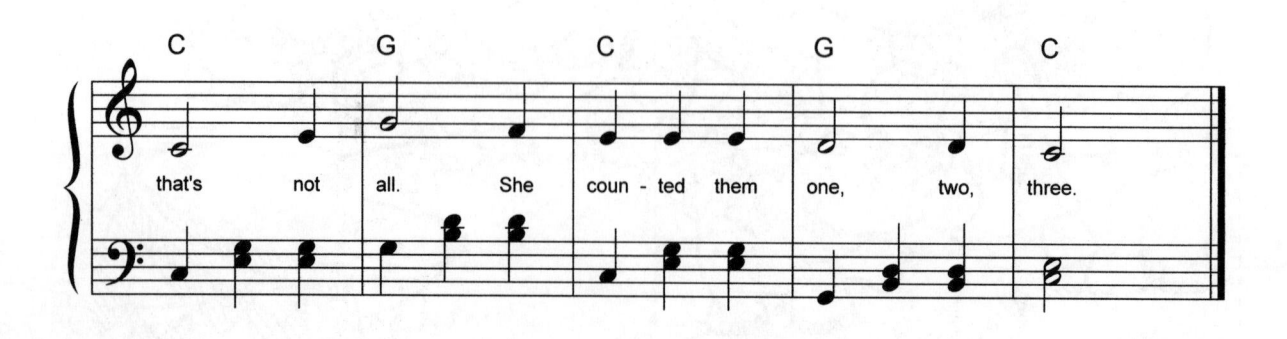

When Goldilocks Went to the House of the Bears

When Goldilocks went to the house of the bears
Oh what did her blue eyes see?
(Children point to their eyes.)

A bowl that was huge, a bowl that was small and a bowl that was tiny and that's not all.
(Children move hands to indicate a 'huge', 'small' and a 'tiny' bowl.)

She counted them one, two, three.
(Children use index finger to count invisible bowls.)

When Goldilocks went to the house of the bears
Oh what did her blue eyes see?
(Children point to their eyes.)

A chair that was huge, a chair that was small and a chair that was tiny and that's not all.
(Children move hands to indicate a 'huge', 'small' and a 'tiny' chair.)

She counted them one, two, three.
(Children use index finger to count invisible chairs.)

When Goldilocks went to the house of the bears
Oh what did her blue eyes see?
(Children point to their eyes.)

A bed that was huge, a bed that was small and a bed that was tiny and that's not all.
(Children move hands to indicate a 'huge', 'small' and 'tiny' bed.)

She counted them one, two, three.
(Children use index finger to count invisible beds.)

When Goldilocks went to the house of the bears
Oh what did her blue eyes see?
(Children point to their eyes.)

A bear that was huge, a bear that was small and a bear that was tiny and that's not all.
(Children use index finger to indicate the height of a 'huge', 'small' and a 'tiny' bear.)

They growled at her one, two, three.
(Children make a growling noise.)

Wild animals

When Goldilocks Went to the House of the Bears

How to use this song

Learning objectives

Stepping Stone
Use size language such as 'big' and 'little'.

Early Learning Goal
Use language such as 'greater', 'smaller', 'heavier' or 'lighter' to compare quantities. **(MD)**

Group size
Six children.

Props
Bowls.
Teddy bears.
Dolls' house, chairs and beds – all in three sizes.

Sharing the song

Use the song for developing concepts of ordering by size, relativity of size, and personal safety, in themes such as 'Large and small' and 'Looking after myself'.

An appropriate time to sing the song is when children are engaged in role-play in the home area. Add three bears, in different sizes, and substitute the name of a child for 'Goldilocks', and names of items in the area, for example, 'A bag that was huge…'.

At the introductory stage, ask everyone to sing along to the CD. Hold up the sets of items, pointing out their sizes. As you hold up each item, ask everyone to sing themselves, according to what you hold up.

Give each child a copy of the photocopiable sheet and ask them to cut out the pictures of the bowls, spoons, mugs and plates. You may need to help, especially with the baby size pictures. Encourage the children to stick them in the right places on the bears' table. Use appropriate size words to describe the items.

Activity ideas

● Talk about whether or not Goldilocks should have been in the forest by herself, and how the children think she came to be there. Ask whether she should have gone inside someone else's house, eaten their food, broken a chair and slept in one of their beds. Say that it is fun sometimes to think of a different ending for a story. Suggest that when the bears came home and found Goldilocks, they were worried that she was lost and wanted to help her. Ask what they could do. **(PSED)**

● Using other 'size' words such as 'big', 'large', 'enormous', 'middle-sized', 'medium', 'standard', 'regular', 'little', 'miniature', 'mini' as the children play. Make collections of three items, such as toy cars, building bricks or dolls, in a row to enable the children to understand the relative different sizes. Invite them to place three teddy bears of differing sizes in size order, asking them to explain their reasons. **(MD)**

● Use adults, children and objects to demonstrate the concept of relativity of size by pointing out that a child standing next to an adult looks small but, if the adult goes away and the child stands next to a plastic spider, the child looks tall. Use examples connected with the song, for example, say that daddy bear's bed was huge. Ask whether it would still look huge if it were next to a giant's bed. **(MD)**

● Play the song softly in the background as one or two children play with a dolls' house containing a table with three play dough bowls in appropriate sizes, three different-sized chairs, beds and bears and a 'Goldilocks'. **(CD)**

Wild animals

When Goldilocks Went to the House of the Bears

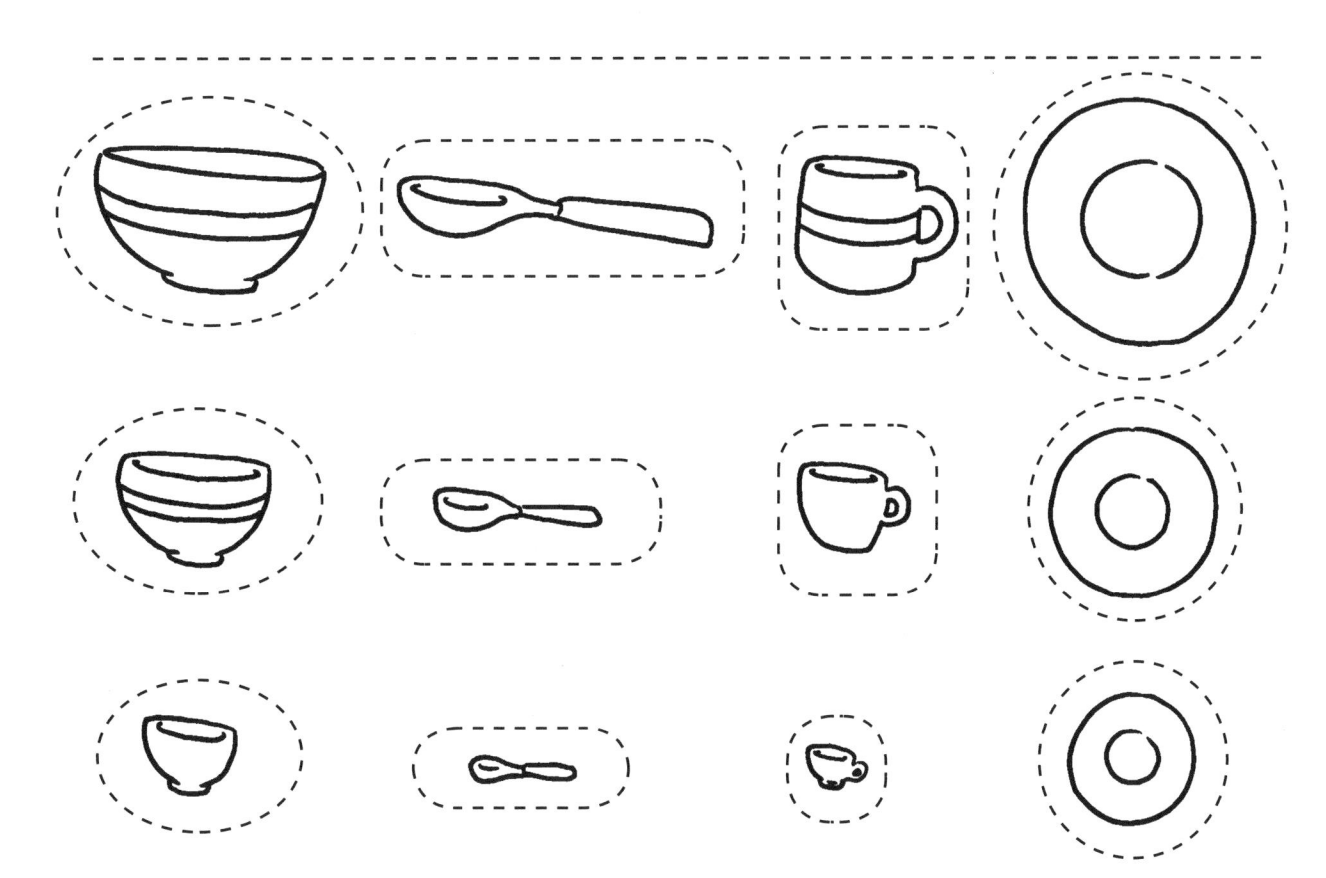

FUN SONGS for the early years: Animal songs

Scholastic Photocopiable

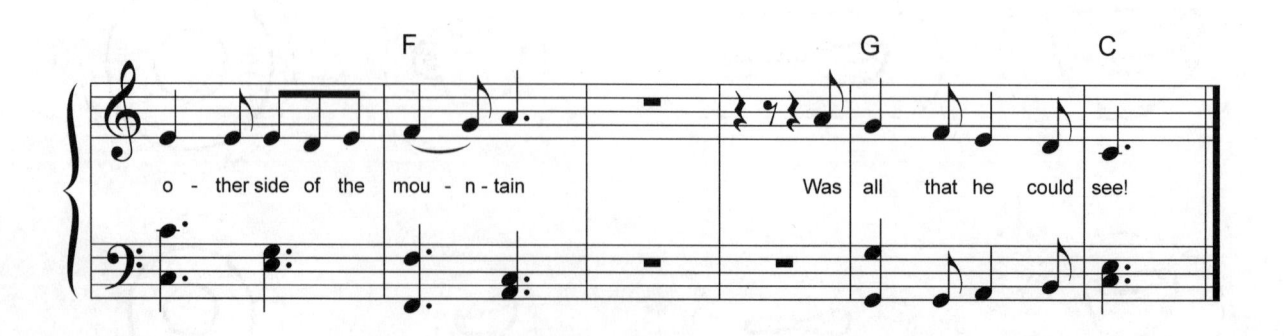

The Bear Went over the Mountain

Oh the bear went o-ver the moun-tain. The bear went o-ver the moun-tain. The bear went o-ver the mou-n-tain to see what he could see! But the o-ther side of the moun-tain, the o-ther side of the moun-tain, the o-ther side of the mou-n-tain Was all that he could see!

Wild animals

The Bear Went over the Mountain

Oh, the bear went over the mountain.
(Children 'walk' the fingers of one hand up the incline of an imaginary mountain.)

The bear went over the mountain.
(As above.)

The bear went over the mountain
(As above.)

to see what he could see!
(Children put one hand over their eyes, to indicate the bear's gaze into the distance.)

But the other side of the mountain,
(Children point, to indicate the other side of the mountain.)

the other side of the mountain,
(As above.)

the other side of the mountain
(As above.)

Was all that he could see!
(Children spread out both arms in an expansive gesture.)

Wild animals

The Bear Went over the Mountain
How to use this song

Learning objectives

Stepping Stone
Examine objects and living things to find out more about them.

Early Learning Goal
Find out about, and identify, some features of living things, objects and events they observe. **(KUW)**

Group size
One child 'bear climber' at a time, with rest of group watching.

Props
Items of climbing gear, if possible, or a child's woolly hat, gloves, sunglasses, rucksack, map, binoculars, climbing rope (skipping rope without handles), 'crampon' (drawn on card), Blu-Tack.

Sharing the song

This song is useful in helping children develop an understanding of the concepts of specialist equipment for a purpose (such as rock climbing), making up a story, pulling forces and skiing. These concepts may form part of themes such as 'Sports and hobbies', 'We like stories', 'Let's move', and 'Holidays and winter'. A good time to sing it is whenever children are using a climbing frame, either inside or outside.

To introduce the song, encourage everyone to sing along to the CD. Show some mountaineering clothes and equipment. If possible, arrange a visit by a rock climber. Invite one child to be a 'mountaineer' who wears appropriate clothing. Ask everyone to sing again as the 'mountaineer' pretends to climb with great care, reach the 'summit', take out binoculars, and survey 'the other side'.

Activity ideas

● Encourage the children to make up stories about how the bear discovered a secret door in the mountain side, and opened it, and had an adventure inside the mountain. **(CLL)**

● Hook one end of a plank (the 'mountain') to the lowest rung of a climbing frame. Securely tie a short skipping rope to the rung above the plank. With Blu-Tack, attach an A4 piece of white card, on which is drawn a crampon, next to the rope, so that the rope looks as though the bear climber has attached it to a mountainside using a crampon (see illustration below). Children, wearing a few items of 'climbing gear', one at a time, pretend to be 'climbing bears'. Hold on to the higher end of the rope yourself, while each 'bear' in turn holds on to the other end, and pulls him/ herself 'up the mountain'. **(PD)**

● Sing 'The skiers skied down the mountain' and so on ending the first verse with 'So they could have some fun'. Let children build a 'mountain' in the sand area, then cover it with a white plastic tablecloth. Children can make skiers by attaching play people to lollipop sticks (skis) with Blu-Tack, and attaching pieces of straw (ski-sticks), also with Blu-Tack. Let children make a ski-lift from junk materials. **(KUW)**